Green Anoles

and Other Pet Lizards

Editorial:
Editor in Chief: Paul A. Kobasa
Project Manager: Cassie Mayer
Writer: Robert Chesbro
Researcher: Cheryl Graham
Manager, Contracts & Compliance
  (Rights & Permissions): Loranne K. Shields
Indexer: David Pofelski

Graphics and Design:
Manager: Tom Evans
Coordinator, Design Development and
  Production: Brenda B. Tropinski
Senior Designer: Isaiah Sheppard
Contributing Photographs Editor: Clover Morell
Cartographer: John Rejba

Pre-Press and Manufacturing:
Director: Carma Fazio
Manufacturing Manager:
  Steven K. Hueppchen
Production/Technology Manager:
  Anne Fritzinger

For information about other World Book publications,
visit our Web site at http://www.worldbookonline.com
or call 1-800-WORLDBK (967-5325).

For information about sales to schools and libraries,
call 1-800-975-3250 (United States),
or 1-800-837-5365 (Canada).

World Book, Inc.
233 N. Michigan Avenue
Chicago, IL 60601
U.S.A.

Library of Congress Cataloging-in-Publication Data
Green anoles and other pet lizards.
    p. cm. — (World Book's animals of the world)
  Includes index.
  Summary: "An introduction to green anoles and other
  pet lizards, presented in a highly illustrated, question-
  and-answer format. Features include fun facts,
  glossary, resource list, index, and scientific
  classification list"—Provided by publisher.
  ISBN 978-0-7166-1368-8
  1. Lizards as pets—Juvenile literature. 2. Anoles—
Juvenile literature. I. World Book, Inc.
SF459.L5G69 2010
639.3'9548—dc22
                                         2009020162

World Book's Animals of the World
Set 6: ISBN: 978-0-7166-1365-7
Printed in China by Leo Paper Products LTD., Heshan, Guangdon
1st printing November 2009

Picture Acknowledgments: Cover: © Jupiter Images/Brand X/Alamy Images; © SilverV/iStockphoto; © Austin J. Stevens, Animals Animals; © Brooke Whatnall, Dreamstime; © Fedor Selivanov, Shutterstock.

© Chris Bott, Alamy Images 41; © Robert Clay, Alamy Images 19; © Digital Vision/Alamy Images 59; © Jupiter Images/Brand X/Alamy Images 17; © Jupiter Images/Goodshoot/Alamy Images 9; © Lisa Moore, Alamy Images 7; © Natural Visions/Alamy Images 43; © Photofrenetic/Alamy Images 49; © James Robinson, Animals Animals 37; © Austin J. Stevens, Animals Animals 5, 51; © Dreamstime 3, 53; © Exo-Terra Rainforest Terrarium 21; © iStockphoto 4, 15, 31, 33, 47, 61; © JP Landry 27; © Karen Millward-Alston 55; © Pete Oxford, Nature Picture Library 57; © Frank Siteman, Photo Edit 25; © James H. Robinson, Photo Researchers 39; © Shutterstock 45; © Rob & Ann Simpson, Visuals Unlimited 5, 35.

Illustrations: WORLD BOOK illustration by Roberta Polfus 13. WORLD BOOK illustration by Adam Weiskind 23, 29.

World Book's Animals of the World

Green Anoles
and Other Pet Lizards

WORLD
BOOK

a Scott Fetzer company
Chicago
www.worldbookonline.com

Contents

What Is a Lizard?

A lizard is an animal that usually has a short neck and a long tail. Lizards are reptiles—animals with dry, scaly skin that breathe by using lungs. Other types of reptiles are snakes, crocodiles, and turtles. Lizards are closely related to snakes.

Lizards come in many different sizes, shapes, and colors. The largest living lizards are the Komodo dragons. They can grow to more than 10 feet (3 meters) long and weigh as much as 365 pounds (165 kilograms)! But many kinds of lizards are only a few inches or centimeters long.

Many people keep certain kinds of lizards as pets. Green anoles *(uh NOH lees)* are popular pet lizards in the United States. These small creatures are fun to observe, but they do have needs that are different from pets like dogs and cats. They can also be expensive pets because they need special equipment to give them just the right environment.

A green anole

Is a Lizard the Right Pet for You?

Though lizards and other reptiles can be fun pets for families with older children, they are not good for everyone. Reptiles can carry germs that make people sick. One of the most dangerous germs they carry is a bacterium called salmonella. This bacterium causes salmonella poisoning, which can be deadly. About 70,000 people in the United States get salmonella poisoning from contact with reptiles every year.

If you have younger brothers or sisters or live with elderly members of your family, a pet lizard is not right for you. The Centers for Disease Control in the United States recommends that children under five years old or people with weak immune systems avoid any contact with reptiles.

If your family decides that a pet reptile is still a good option, be sure to wash your hands thoroughly after handling your pet or anything in its cage, and never allow your pet to roam freely throughout your house.

Lizards must be handled with special care.

9

Where Do Green Anoles and Other Lizards Live?

Lizards live on all continents except Antarctica. Most lizards live in hot, tropical areas near the equator. They live in many habitats, including deserts, rain forests, and marshes. Lizards are usually found on the ground or in trees. Some lizards make burrows in the ground.

Green anoles live in areas where the climate is not as hot and humid as it is near the equator. They can be found in the Southern United States from North Carolina to Oklahoma and Texas. Other types of anole are found in regions closer to the equator, such as the West Indies, Central America, and South America.

Green anoles can live in shrubs and grasses around rocks and logs, but they are mainly arboreal *(ahr BAWR ee uhl)*. This means they prefer to live in trees, where they can blend in with leaves and branches.

10

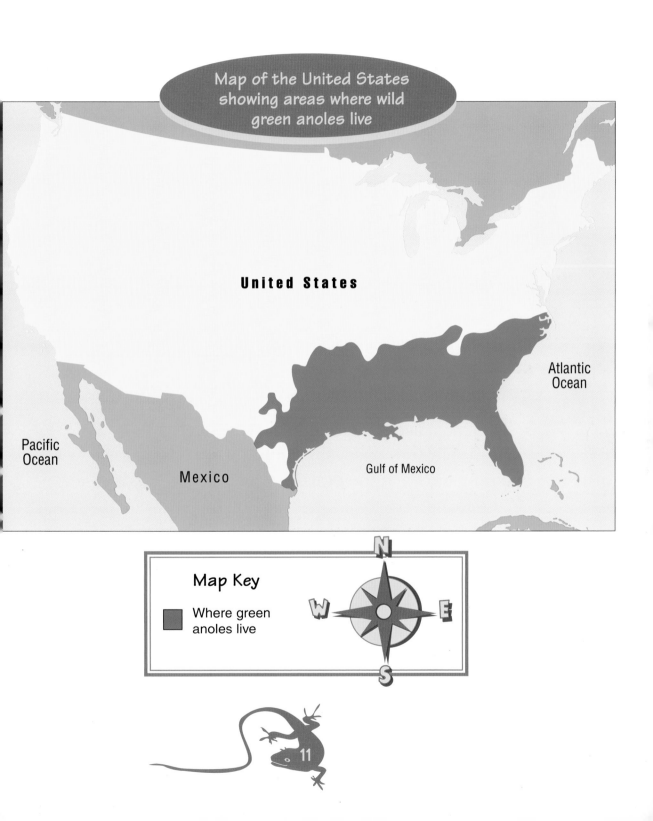

Map of the United States showing areas where wild green anoles live

United States

Atlantic Ocean

Pacific Ocean

Mexico

Gulf of Mexico

Map Key

Where green anoles live

N

W   E

S

11

What Does a Green Anole Look Like?

All lizards are vertebrates *(VUR tuh brihts)*, a group of animals that have backbones. And they all have bodies covered in scales—small, rough plates that protect the animal from attackers.

Green anoles are about 5 to 8 inches (12.7 to 20.3 centimeters) in length. They have long tails that can reach twice the length of their bodies. Their mouths are lined with sharp teeth designed for grabbing and holding prey (animals they hunt).

Like most lizards, green anoles have four short limbs. Anoles are excellent climbers because of their special toes. Each toe ends with a pad and a sharp claw. These pads have thousands of gummy little bristles that stick to the bark of the tree or even to walls of buildings or fence posts.

Green anoles can change color from green to brown. Their color may change with their mood, but it also helps them to blend in with brown trees or green vegetation.

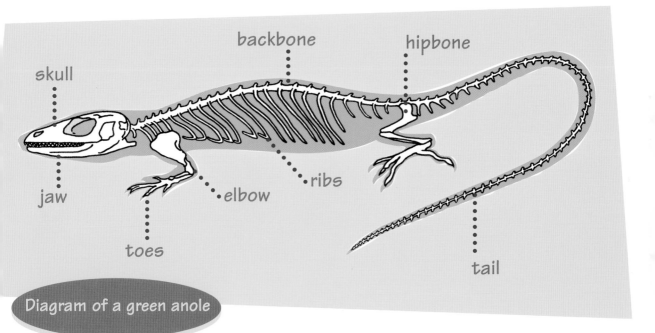

skull

backbone

hipbone

jaw

toes

elbow

ribs

tail

Diagram of a green anole

13

What Does "Cold-blooded" Mean?

Lizards are different from most pets. Pets like dogs, cats, and hamsters are mammals, a type of vertebrate that feeds its young on the mother's milk. Mammals are warm-blooded. Their body temperature stays about the same, even when their surroundings get warmer or colder.

Lizards and other reptiles are cold-blooded. This means their body temperature stays the same as their surroundings. Because of this, lizards live mostly in warm regions, like deserts or tropical rain forests. Most lizards can't survive in places that get too cold because they would freeze to death.

Lizards must constantly work to keep their bodies at the right temperature. They can often be found basking (sun-bathing) in the sun in the morning and hiding in the shade if the temperature rises above 90 °F (32 °C). At nighttime, many lizards hide in burrows because the ground stays warmer than the air.

14

Green anoles bask in the sun to warm their bodies.

15

What Should You Look for When Buying a Green Anole?

A green anole or any other lizard should be purchased from a certified pet store. Qualified pet experts are trained to teach you how to properly care for your anole.

Anoles born in captivity tend to be the healthiest pets. Wild anoles that are captured and then sold to pet stores can be more prone to illness and are not recommended as pets.

When buying a green anole, look for signs of illness. Healthy lizards should look alert and active, and most will try to escape if you reach your hand in the cage to pick them up. A lethargic anole may be sick, or its tank may be too cold. Also, check to make sure your lizard is not too thin, which can also be a sign of illness. If you can see the lizard's hip bones or tail bone, it is probably not a healthy lizard. Loose skin may be a sign that the lizard is dehydrated.

A healthy green anole
should look alert.

What Does a Green Anole Eat?

Anoles are insectivores *(ihn SEHK tuh vawrs)*—that is, they eat insects. They like to eat food that is alive and moving, so giving them dead insects is not a good idea. If you're squeamish around insects, a pet lizard may not be the right choice for you.

Crickets should make up the main part of your anole's diet. Crickets are fairly cheap and can be purchased at a local pet store. You can also feed your anole insects that you catch around the home, as long as they are free of pesticides (chemicals that are used on plants to kill insects). Vitamin powder purchased at a pet store should be sprinkled on crickets so that the anole gets the proper vitamins and minerals in its diet.

Green anoles are usually good eaters, so you can feed them every other day. Your anole should get three to four insects per feeding.

An anole munching on
a cricket

Where Should a Green Anole Be Kept?

An anole's home should be as much like its natural habitat as possible. You should keep your anole in a ventilated glass tank called a terrarium *(tuh RAIR ee uhm)*. A 10-gallon (38-liter) tank standing upright can be used for one or two anoles. Make sure the screen lid on top of your cage is secure to prevent your anole from escaping.

Place branches inside the terrarium to give your anole a perching place. You should also create places to hide inside the cage so your pet can feel safe and secure.

Soil or moss covered with bark, leaves, or mulch is best for the bottom of the terrarium. A few small potted plants should be placed in the tank to create shade and to help keep the environment moist.

Anoles also need special lamps for heat and light. You can read more about these lamps on pages 22 and 24.

20

Terrariums need many places for green anoles to climb and hide.

Why Is Temperature Important?

Green anoles depend on their surroundings for heat because they are cold-blooded. You must create a range of temperatures inside the terrarium to keep your anole healthy. Basking lamps and other heating elements are available at most pet stores and can be used to create the right temperature range.

Measure the temperature of various spots in the tank every day to make sure the temperatures are suitable for your pet. Most parts of the tank should have a daytime temperature range between 75 and 85 °F (24 and 30 °C). One end of the tank should have a basking spot, where the anole can gather sunlight and heat. The basking spot should be 85 to 90 °F (about 30 to 32 °C) during the day.

A temperature of 65 to 75 °F (about 18 to 24 °C) is appropriate for nighttime. If necessary, use a ceramic heating element instead of the heat lamp at night. (The light from the basking lamp will confuse your anole and may cause it to become stressed.)

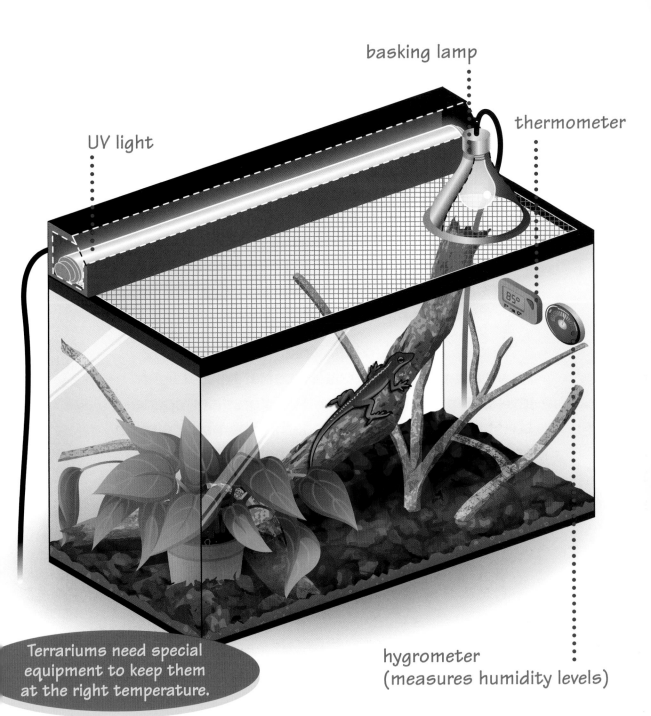

basking lamp

thermometer

UV light

85°

hygrometer
(measures humidity levels)

Terrariums need special
equipment to keep them
at the right temperature.

23

Why Is Light Important?

Just as human beings are awakened by sunlight, green anoles react to light as well. Green anoles need 12 to14 hours of light per day. If anoles do not get the proper amount of light, they may become confused or even sick. Pet stores sell automatic timers, which can be used to make sure your anole gets the right amount of light.

Anoles also need ultraviolet (UV) light for 12 hours per day. UV light is a special type of light invisible to the human eye. Pet stores sell special UV lights that can be attached to the outside of an anole's terrarium, where the anole cannot touch them. An anole can get UV light from sunlight if the terrarium is placed near a window.

Lighting elements should be placed outside the terrarium.

Why Is Humidity Important?

Humidity is a measure of how much water is in the air. Wild anoles live in places with high humidity, which helps to keep them hydrated and healthy. An anole's terrarium should be kept at 60 to 70 percent humidity. Most pet stores sell a simple device called a hygrometer to measure humidity.

It is very important that you mist (spray with water) an anole's home once or twice a day. Mist more often if the air is dry. The water should be as clean and pure as possible.

Though some anoles have been known to drink from water bowls, most will not know what one is. It is best to spray water on the leaves of plants for the anole to lap up.

A green anole perched
on a dewy leaf

How Do You Keep a Terrarium Clean?

A responsible pet owner understands that a few small tasks must be performed each day to make sure an anole's home is safe and clean. Any uneaten insects and droppings should be removed from the tank, and any water droplets on the glass of the tank should be wiped off. The tank should be misted at least twice a day and temperatures should be carefully checked.

Other jobs should be done at least once a week, such as cleaning your pet's food container. The tank must also be cleaned. Make sure the tank is dry before placing the anole back in it. A smaller tank can be purchased for holding the anole while its larger tank is cleaned.

Also, the lamps, heating elements, and timers must be checked to make sure they're working properly.

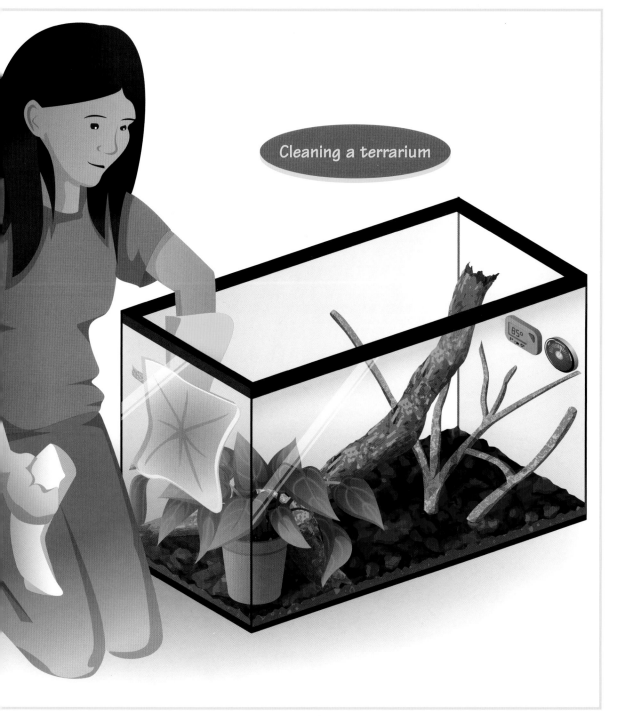

Cleaning a terrarium

29

How Should You Handle a Green Anole?

Like any pet, a green anole should be handled with extreme care. Most anoles do not like being picked up, but it may be necessary to do so from time to time, such as when you clean your pet's terrarium.

Move slowly when you pick up your anole. Place your thumb and forefinger just behind its head and gently squeeze it (not too hard!). This will prevent the anole from turning its head and biting you. You can then gently wrap your hand around the anole and pick it up. Never pick up your anole by the tail because it might fall off!

If an anole bites, it is natural for you to want to pull your hand away. This can be very harmful to the anole if its mouth is still clamped down on your skin. Anole bites usually do not hurt, so try not to pull your hand away until the anole lets go.

Always wash your hands before and after handling your anole or anything in its cage.

Be gentle when holding
your pet anole.

Why Do Green Anoles Have a Fan on Their Throat?

One of the most interesting features of anoles is their throat fan, or dewlap. The dewlap is a colorful fold of skin, usually bright pink with spots, underneath the chin or neck of the lizard. It is barely visible unless inflated.

Male anoles inflate and deflate their dewlaps to attract mates. While doing so, they may also bob their heads or lift their bodies up and down, like they're doing push-ups.

Male anoles also inflate their dewlaps for self-defense against predators (animals that hunt them), or when they are competing with other males during mating season. A caged male may inflate its dewlap if it feels threatened or if it is not yet comfortable in its home.

32

A male green anole inflates his dewlap.

Why Do Green Anoles Change Color?

Scientists don't know the exact reason why green anoles change color. An anole may change color to control its temperature. It is usually green during the day. At night it may change to brown because brown absorbs heat better than green.

Caged anoles turn brown from the stress of being handled in their cages, or due to poor nutrition or too little humidity. Anoles in the wild may turn brown when threatened by predators or other competing anoles during the mating season.

Unlike chameleons, anoles cannot control when they change color. But an anole's color usually blends in well with its environment, such as green plants or brown vegetation.

34

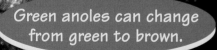

Green anoles can change
from green to brown.

How Do Green Anoles Escape Attackers?

Green anoles and some other kinds of lizards have a special talent. If an attacker grabs their tail, it falls off! The tail is often still moving, which helps to distract the predator while the lizard makes a quick getaway. Later, the lizard grows a new tail, but it is usually not as long as the original tail and may be less colorful.

The new tail can take anywhere from a few months to a few years to grow back. Big lizards like iguanas and Komodo dragons may lose their tail in a fight, but the tail does not grow back.

Though lizards aren't gravely harmed when they perform their "tail trick," you should never grab a lizard by the tail. Tails are very important to lizards in the wild. They can help to balance the lizard. In addition, a lizard's tail stores fat, an important source of energy.

36

Green anoles can grow
new tails.

Why Do Green Anoles Shed Their Skin?

If you keep a green anole or other lizard, you may observe a layer of their skin coming off from time to time. This is completely normal. Like most lizards, anoles shed as they grow. Younger anoles shed more frequently than older anoles because they are still growing. Older anoles shed only a few times per year.

Some lizards shed their skin all at once, so it comes off in one big piece. Anoles shed their skin in smaller pieces. An anole may shed without its owner noticing because it eats the skin it sheds! It does so because the skin is filled with nutrients that help to keep the anole healthy.

An anole's skin may become duller in color before it sheds, and the animal may seem less active and have less of an appetite. These are normal behaviors for a shedding anole, but they can also be symptoms of illness. If your pet still seems lethargic a few days after shedding and does not regain its appetite, take it to the vet.

An anole sheds
its skin.

What Are Other Kinds of Anoles?

Anole is the name of about 300 species (kinds) of lizards that live in the West Indies and in Central and South America. The green anole is native to the Southern United States. Other kinds of anoles include the knight anole, brown anole, and bark anole.

The knight anole is the largest kind of anole, growing to a length of 13 to 20 inches (33 to 51 centimeters). It is bright green with a yellow or white stripe underneath the eye and across the shoulder. The knight anole is native to Cuba but is now found in some parts of Florida.

The brown anole is originally from the Caribbean, but it has also been introduced to Florida. This small creature is always some shade of brown or gray and usually has white or yellow patterns on the back.

The bark anole is another Caribbean lizard that has been introduced to Florida. Bark anoles are brown with patterns that look like tree bark, making these lizards nearly impossible to spot in their habitat.

40

A knight anole

What Are Other Kinds of Pet Lizards?

There are thousands of different species of lizards, but only a few kinds make suitable pets. Some lizards are too large to keep as pets, some are too dangerous, and some are illegal to own.

Along with green anoles, iguanas *(ih GWAH nuhs)* and geckos *(GEHK ohs)* are the most common lizards kept as pets. Iguanas are large lizards that require much space. Geckos are relatively small and easy to care for.

The following pages describe some of the kinds of lizards that people keep as pets. Some lizards are considered easier to care for than green anoles, but others are recommended only for experienced lizard owners. Before purchasing your lizard, be sure to learn all you can about its care so you will know if it's the right pet for you.

A Chinese water dragon

What Is a Gecko?

A gecko is a fascinating pet that is popular among lizard owners. Most geckos grow 4 to 6 inches (10 to 15 centimeters) long. Some can live for a very long time—up to 30 years! Scientists have identified over 1,000 different species of geckos.

Like anoles, geckos are excellent climbers and have flat, sticky toe pads. The toe pads make it very easy for them to climb vertical (upright) surfaces. Because geckos are such good climbers, they are also very good at escaping from their cages and can be very difficult to catch because they are so fast. Geckos may also bite when handled.

Unlike other lizards, geckos are "talkative." They can be heard making chirping sounds when communicating with other lizards.

In some ways, geckos are easier to care for than other lizards because they don't need a special UV light.

A gecko

What Is an Iguana?

An iguana is a kind of lizard that lives in dry areas like deserts, although a few species live in rain forests. Green iguanas are the most common kind of iguana that is kept as a pet. These lizards can be quite large, growing to 6 feet (1.8 meters) long! They range in color from gray to green, with brown bands around the body and tail.

Green iguanas have a striking appearance. They have a spiny crest of scales down their back and tail. They also have a dewlap, which they will display when threatened or when mating. Their long, sharp claws help them to climb trees. Unlike most other lizards, green iguanas eat mainly plants.

Wild green iguanas have become threatened because they are captured and sold as pets. Many people breed green iguanas in captivity and sell them as pets, but these lizards can have health problems because they breed only with a small group of lizards. Also, if they are bred in other countries, they may carry diseases. Many people feel that green iguanas should not be kept as pets because they are so difficult to keep healthy.

A green iguana

What Is a Chameleon?

Chameleons *(kuh MEE lee uhns)* are a large group of lizards that some experienced lizard owners keep as pets. Most chameleons live in the forests of mainland Africa and on the African island country of Madagascar.

Chameleons are famous for changing color. For example, chameleons that are green or yellow may suddenly change to brown or black if they become scared.

Chameleons move extremely slowly, almost like they are in slow motion. Their eyes are like small globes, each moving separately from the other. Many species have a tail that can grasp objects, such as tree branches. Chameleons also have long, sticky tongues that they use to quickly snatch insects.

Chameleons are expensive to buy and very delicate. A chameleon can get stressed easily, perhaps so badly that it may die. Many people believe that chameleons should not be kept as pets. Though a chameleon pet is for experienced lizard owners only, it may be best for the chameleon to remain in the wild.

48

A chameleon

What Is a Blue-tongued Skink?

One of the more unusual pet lizards is the blue-tongued skink. As their name suggests, these creatures have a bright blue tongue, which they stick out of their mouths when bothered!

Most pet blue-tongued skinks are native to the forests, woodlands, and grasslands of Northern Australia, New Guinea, and some other Pacific islands. They are ground-dwelling animals that feed on insects, snails, flowers, and fruits during the day. At night, they hide in hollow logs or underneath plant matter.

Blue-tongued skinks measure from 1 to 2 feet (30 to 61 centimeters) long. Their bodies are long and flat, which helps them to move underground.

Blue-tongued skinks are usually gentle and easy to tame. However, they need fairly large tanks with areas for them to burrow and hide.

50

A blue-tongued skink

What Is a Bearded Dragon?

A bearded dragon is a medium-sized lizard native to Australia. Bearded dragons grow to between 13 and 24 inches (33 to 61 centimeters) long from head to tail. The kinds of bearded dragons most commonly sold as pets live in dry, rocky areas. They range in color from dull brown to tan with red or gold highlights.

Bearded dragons get their name from their "beard"—a dewlap with spiky scales that encircles their throat. They expand their dewlap to make themselves look tough in front of other lizards. Male bearded dragons also do so to impress females.

Bearded dragons are considered quite sociable. Some bearded dragons even "greet" other lizards (or their owners) by standing on three legs and waving one front leg in a circular motion. Scientists believe that wild bearded dragons do so to show that they recognize or admit defeat to another lizard.

A bearded dragon

What Kinds of Fun Can You Have with Your Green Anole?

People can form strong bonds with pets like cats and dogs, but a lizard is a different kind of pet. It is unlikely that your green anole will show affection toward you, and it may never be comfortable when you hold it. But lizards are fascinating creatures to observe.

A fun thing to do is to slowly and carefully lower a mirror in front of your anole. The anole will see its reflection and inflate its dewlap, thinking it sees another anole. You may also enjoy putting a live moth or other winged insect into the cage and watch your anole hunt its prey.

You can have fun with your anole, as long as you are sensitive to its needs. It might be helpful to think of your anole as a pet fish—only for looking at.

Green anoles can see their reflection.

What Are Some Common Signs of Illness in a Green Anole?

As a rule, a green anole is a healthy anole, and a brown anole is a stressed anole. A green anole will naturally change from green to brown and back, but if a green anole is brown for a very long time, it may be very sick. A sick anole may become sluggish and stop moving. It may even stop eating.

Many things can stress an anole to the point where it becomes ill. Cats and dogs staring at it may cause stress. Extreme changes in humidity, temperature, and light may also cause serious harm to an anole. Other anoles in a cage may cause stress as well.

Signs of a very sick anole are deep skin wrinkles from dehydration, black spots behind the eyes, or lumps on the side of the neck. If your anole has any of these symptoms, call your veterinarian immediately.

Weight loss can be a sign of illness in green anoles.

What Routine Veterinary Care Is Needed?

If possible, you should bring your new pet anole to be examined by a vet for disease and parasites. Parasites are microscopic creatures that may cause illness in the anole, the owner, or the owner's family.

Anoles require very little routine veterinary care, but it is wise to know of a local lizard specialist in advance in case your anole becomes sick. An owner should make sure an anole is eating and moving properly. The owner should also make sure it is shedding on a regular basis, especially in the area around the nose and toes.

Some vets are specially trained to care for lizards.

What Are Your Responsibilities as an Owner?

It may seem strange, but to the anole its owner may seem like a giant predator. A good owner should be gentle and sensitive to the unique needs of his or her anole. You must check your anole and its environment every day.

Heat, light, humidity, water, and proper nutrition are the most important factors in keeping an anole healthy. It is also important to protect the anole from as much stress as possible.

If cared for properly, an anole can live a long and healthy life, usually about 4 to 7 years. An owner should feel proud to keep a healthy pet lizard and have the chance to learn about how it behaves.

An anole perching among leaves

Lizard Fun Facts

→ The Komodo dragon is the largest living lizard. It grows to more than 10 feet (3 meters) long and weighs up to 365 pounds (165 kilograms). Komodo dragons can kill deer, wild pigs, and water buffaloes. They have even killed humans that get too close!

→ The horned lizard has an unusual way of defending itself. It sprays a high-pressure stream of blood from its eyes to scare away predators!

→ Iguanas sneeze just like humans do, and for the same reasons. But unlike humans, iguanas sneeze salt because they do not want it in their bodies.

→ The Gila monster has a poisonous bite that it uses to defend itself against other animals. The bites are painful but not deadly to people.

Glossary

arboreal Living in or among trees.

breed To produce animals by carefully selecting and mating them for certain traits.

burrow A hole dug in the ground by an animal for shelter. Also, to dig a hole in the ground.

cold-blooded Having a body temperature that stays the same as the air temperature.

dewlap The flap of skin around the neck of some lizards.

habitat Where an animal lives.

insectivore An animal that eats insects.

mammal A type of animal that feeds its young with milk made by the mother.

parasite An organism (living creature) that feeds on and lives on or in the body of another organism, often causing harm to the being on which it feeds.

predator An animal that hunts other animals for food.

prey An animal hunted for food.

reptiles A group of cold-blooded animals that have scaly skin and usually reproduce by laying eggs.

shed To throw off or lose hair, skin, fur, or other body covering.

terrarium A glass or plastic container in which small plants or small land animals are kept.

tropical An area of Earth that is near the equator.

ultraviolet light (UV) A type of invisible light coming from the sun that animals need to stay alive. UV rays cause sunburns.

vertebrate An animal with a backbone.

warm-blooded Having warm blood or blood that stays about the same temperature regardless of the air or water around the animal.

Index

(Boldface indicates a photo, map, or illustration.)

For more information about green anoles and other lizards, try these resources:

Books:
All About Lizards by Jim Arnosky (Scholastic, 2004)
Fun Facts About Lizards by Carmen Bredeson (Enslow Elementary, 2008)
Lizards: Weird and Wonderful by Margery Facklam and Alan Male (Little, Brown, 2003)
The Pebble First Guide to Lizards by Zachary Pitts (Capstone Press, 2009)

Web sites:
Lizard care
http://www.lizard-care.com
National Geographic: Reptiles Index
http://animals.nationalgeographic.com/animals/reptiles.html
Reptile Channel: Kid Corner
http://www.reptilechannel.com/kid-corner/default.aspx
San Diego Zoo's Animal Bytes: Lizard
http://www.sandiegozoo.org/animalbytes/t-lizard.html

Lizard Classification

Scientists classify animals by placing them into groups. The animal kingdom is a group that contains all the world's animals. Phylum, class, order, and family are smaller groups. Each phylum contains many classes. A class contains orders, an order contains families, and a family contains genuses. One or more species belong to each genus. Each species has its own scientific name. Here is how the animals in this book fit into this system.

Animals with backbones and their relatives (Phylum Chordata)
Reptiles (Class Reptilia)
Lizards and snakes (Order Squamata)

Beaded lizards (Family Helodermatidae)
Mexican beaded lizard . . . .*Heloderma horridum*
Gila monster . . . .*Heloderma suspectum*

Casque-headed lizards (Family Corytophanidae)
Helmeted lizards . . . .*Corytophanes* spp.

Chameleons (Family Chamaeleonidae)
Jackson's chameleon . . . .*Chamaeleo jacksonii*
Panther chameleon . . . .*Chamaeleo (furcifer) pardalis*

Geckos (Family Gekkonidae)
Dwarf gecko . . . .*Sphaerodactylus ariasae*
Tokay gecko . . . .*Gekko gecko*

Glass lizards and their relatives (Family Anguidae)
Glass lizards . . . .*Ophisaurus* spp.

Girdle-tailed lizards (Family Cordylidae)
Armadillo lizard . . . .*Cordylus cataphractus*
Sungazer . . . .*Cordylus giganteus*

Iguanas and their relatives (Family Iguanidae)
Anoles . . . .*Anolis* spp.*
Basilisks . . . .*Basiliscus* spp.**
Chuckwallas . . . .*Sauromalus* spp.
Coachella Valley fringe-toed lizard . . . .*Uma inornata****
Collared lizards . . . .*Crotaphytus* spp.****
Desert iguana . . . .*Dipsosaurus dorsalis*
Fiji crested iguana . . . .*Brachylophus vitiensis*
Galapagos land iguana . . . .*Conolophus subcristatus*
Galapagos marine iguana . . . .*Amblyrhynchus cristatus*
Green, or common, iguana . . . .*Iguana iguana*
Horned lizards . . . .*Phrynosoma* spp.***

Monitor lizards (Family Varanidae)
Komodo dragon . . . .*Varanus komodoensis*

Old World lizards (Family Agamidae)
Bearded lizard . . . .*Pogona vitticeps*
Flying dragons . . . .*Draco* spp.
Frilled lizard . . . .*Chlamydosaurus kingii*

Skinks (Family Scincidae)

Whiptails (Family Teiidae)
Six-lined racerunner . . . .*Cnemidophorus sexlineatus*
Spotted whiptail . . . .*Cnemidophorus exsanguis*

* Some scientists classify certain of these lizards under the genus *Norops*. May also be grouped in the family Polychrotidae.

** May be grouped into the family Corytophanidae.

*** May be grouped into the family Phrynosonmatidae.

**** May be grouped into the family Crotaphytidae.